KETO FOODS

LOW CARBS
VEGETABLES
GOOD MEATS
HEALTHY FATS
SEAFOOD & FISH

4 Ingredients KETO

4 Ingredients
PO Box 400
Caloundra QLD 4551
+61 7 5341 8282

ABN: **17 435 679 521**

🌐   4ingredients.com.au

f   facebook.com/4ingredientspage

▶   4 ingredients Channel

🐦   @4ingredients

℗   @4ingredients

📷   4 Ingredients

✉   info@4ingredients.com.au

Published by 4 Ingredients July 2019

The moral right of the Author has been asserted.

Photography:	www.4ingredients.com.au
Design & Formatting:	Shem Hunter; www.shemhunterdesign.com
Publisher:	4 Ingredients
Distribution:	Simon & Schuster, Australia
	Simon & Schuster, New Zealand
ISBN:	978-0-6484851-1-7

Every effort has been made to ensure the information contained in this book is complete and accurate.

The information in this publication is representative of the author's opinions and views. It is meant for educational and informational purposes only, and is not meant to prevent, diagnose, treat or cure any disease. The content should not be construed as professional medical advice.

The Author is not responsible for any specific health or allergy needs that may require medical supervision and is not responsible for any adverse reactions to the recipes within.

Should the reader need professional assistance, a qualified physician or health care practitioner should be consulted.

What is KETO?

A KETOGENIC DIET is a strict regime of High Fat Low Carb (HFLC) that turns your body into a state of **KETOSIS. Ketosis** is where you burn fat instead of carbohydrates for energy.

Successfully following a Keto-diet convinces our bodies to act metabolically as if it was starving even as we take in enough calories and nutrition to remain healthy. A properly formulated ketogenic diet should have high fat, moderate protein and low carbohydrate intake.

As a general rule a traditional keto diet with a standard **Fat : Protein : Carb ratio, is 75 : 20 : 5.**

NB: You will see that not all the recipes within follow this exact formula, but many Dinners for example, assume you will add sides and sauces to them which will weigh into the ratio. As with all new diets, consult a specialist before you start, to ensure a menu plan that will provide the best possible outcome for you.

Keto Diet in 1920
The Keto diet was originally developed for children with epilepsy. This diet dates back to the 1920s when doctors in Washington D.C figured out that forcing children with epilepsy into ketosis, through a low carb diet, appeared to reduce seizures.

Melanie Bohemer, a registered dietitian at Lenox Hill Hospital in NYC says "We have used very low carbohydrate diets to treat epileptics in a clinical setting for a very, very long time. Now is the first time we are seeing it used by more general populations for weight management."

LIVELOVEKETO

Why KETO?

If you have followed food-trends of late you would most definitely have heard of KETO!

The High Fat Low Carb (HFLC) method of eating has captivated popular culture and more people than ever people are wondering whether it will make a difference to their health?

Most doctors advocate that a healthy diet, along with stress management techniques such as sleep and exercise are best for balanced lifestyles.

Many health professionals also believe eating a clean, ketogenic diet will help.

Start small and learn how first. Anyone who has succeeded at the Ketogenic Diet will know that the secret to success is careful planning and preparation.

Recently, Liz, a lady who has followed my own Keto journey on Social Media, contacted us. Living with cancer, her oncologist suggested she start following a **KETO** diet. This is the Article Summary from www.thetruthaboutcancer.com/ketogenic-diet-weakens-cancer-cells she was sent; compelling reading.

- Research continues to show that sugar is the main source of fuel which feeds cancer and contributes to an inflammatory environment.

- A low carbohydrate diet produces a metabolic state known as ketosis. This is a process in which the body burns ketones to make energy, instead of relying on sugar or carbohydrates.

- You can effectively produce ketones by limiting the carbohydrates in your diet to less than 80 grams daily and protein to no more than 1.2 grams of protein/per kg lean body mass.

- Carbohydrates are broken down into glucose which feeds cancer cells. By removing carbohydrates from your diet, you can also deplete cancer cells of their energy supply. The lowest survival rate in cancer patients is among those with the highest blood sugar levels.

- The ketogenic diet is particularly effective when combined with periods of intermittent fasting. Fasting increases ketone production and can starve cancer cells.

- Diets high in protein can also feed cancer. A moderate protein diet is recommended on the ketogenic diet. You can starve cancer by practicing a ketogenic diet consisting of an abundance of healthy fats (about 75 percent), 20 percent protein, and no more than 5 percent carbohydrates.

- Supplementing with high quality (non-synthetic) multivitamins, probiotics, and omega-3s is also recommended on a ketogenic diet.

Is KETO for me?

1. Would you love an easy way to burn fat?

2. Don't want to give up delicious foods like cheese and bacon?
   In fact, you want a daily diet that encourages the consumption of meat and dairy.

3. The theory is to get your body to replace **KETONES** by eating less than 20g of carbohydrates/day. **Ketones** are chemicals made in your liver. You produce them when you don't have enough insulin in your body to turn sugar (or glucose) into energy. You need another source, so your body uses fat instead.

4. This allows your body to essentially run entirely on fat; allowing it to access fat stores (eg. the belly) and burn it off.

5. Sounds great right?

6. Well there are a couple of things to keep in mind ...

7. Those with diabetes or high blood pressure should avoid this diet.

8. The diet may also be low in vitamins, depending on what you eat, so you may need to add health supplements.

9. Studies have shown that the Keto diet can improve mental performance and increase physical endurance.

10. Are you ready to turn your body into a fat burning machine?

IF THIS IS YOU?
Always consult a qualified medical professional before beginning any nutritional program. Low-carb diets can have unpleasant side-effects for some, including constipation, bad breath and headaches. They can also lead to poor energy levels and fatigue, making exercise difficult to undertake. What is right for some, may not be for others.

KETO diets are great and even easy, but only if you do these two simple things...

Researching content and recipes for this book, I followed and subscribed to many websites and blogs. One of the most interesting was a site called Keto Summit www.ketosummit.com.

Run by a husband (Jeremy) and wife (Louise) team who have been helping people with diet and nutrition for a very long time, I read an article called "Why Keto fails for some people?" https://ketosummit.com/o1-keto-diet.

Here is an extract I found really interesting, it may help you too?

1.   **Avoid inflammatory foods – even ones that are low-carb.**

This is one of those things that many "experts" either don't know or just forget to tell you. But it's incredibly important. You can lose weight and heal your body while eating foods like Chocolate Fat Bombs, and Strawberry Chia Puddings. But you will not get great results if you're still eating inflammatory foods. It just won't work. In particular, you must avoid seed oils and even dairy.

And I know you don't want to give up your cheese. But the truth is that most people become inflamed when they eat dairy. And that inflammation will stall your weight loss and keep you from getting healthy. Think proteins and lots of vegetables for best results.

2.   **Faster, Simpler and Easier – you CANNOT pretend that you'll have more time or willpower than you really will.**

This sounds so obvious. Doesn't everyone want to make their life faster, simpler, and easier?

The problem is that you get excited or determined, and you start planning to cook gourmet meals, to go to the gym every morning, and to never eat another cookie.

And while those are worthy goals, it's almost impossible to stick to them for a long time.

You might have to work late one night, your kids might get sick, or you could just be tired and irritable one day. In other words, life happens.

But the fact is - you already know the solution - instead of relying on willpower or luck, you must surround yourself with delicious Keto foods that are fast, simple, and easy.

It's honestly that simple.

As with life and all types of diets, you read an article that tells you **why?** And then an article which tells you **why not?** Although I found this article as to why Keto diets don't work for some (because it made sense to me) I have still included recipes that contain cheese. In many eg., Herbed Omlette P. 33 and Asparagus Wraps P. 47 it can easily be omitted. Include or omit cheese depending on how your keto journey is progressing.

Being healthy isn't easy, and a KETO diet, may or may not be for everyone. As with all things, before you commence a new diet, consult your dietitian, nutritionist or GP for help and guidance to develop a healthy, balanced diet for you. If a KETO diet is recommended, please use this cookbook in consultation with your GP to create a menu plan that best suits you and your current situation.

KETO Friendly Foods
HIGH FAT LOW CARB (HFLC)

MEAT
Bacon

Beef (lean mince, steak etc.)

Beef jerky

Chicken

Duck

Lamb (chops, backstrap, roast etc.)

Pork (chops, bacon, shoulders etc.)

Veal

SEAFOOD
Anchovies

Calamari

Mussels

Oysters

Prawns (Shrimp)

Salmon

Sardines

Shellfish

Tuna (fresh & tinned)

NB: *Apart from organ meats, shellfish is the most nutrient-dense food you can eat. Often expensive, but worth it.*

CONDIMENTS
Avocado oil

Capers

Dijon Mustard

HEINZ No-Added Sugar Ketchup

Hot Sauce
Made from vinegar, chilli and a touch of seasoning.

Lemon & Lime Juice
Don't discount the impact a splash of fresh lemon or lime juice can have on your meals especially when paired with fresh herbs.

Newman's OWN Caesar Dressing

Newman's OWN Classic Oil & Vinegar Dressing

Newman's OWN Italian Dressing

Sea Salt (in moderation)

Sugar-free Tomato Sauce

Tamari Soy Sauce

Whole-egg Mayonnaise

Yellow mustard

PANTRY ITEMS
Almond meal (flour)

Coconut flour

Coconut oil

Gluten free Tamari Sauce

Nut flours
(eg. walnut, hazelnut)

Psyllium husk

Tahini (sesame)

HERBS & SPICES
Check the ingredients of any herb or spice blends to avoid added sugar or MSG.

Sea Salt

Black Pepper

White Pepper

Basil

Italian Seasoning

Chilli Powder

Cayenne Pepper

Curry Powder

Garlic Powder

Garam Masala

Cumin

Oregano

Thyme

Rosemary

Sage

Turmeric

Parsley

Cilantro

Cinnamon

Nutmeg

Cloves

Allspice

Ginger

Cardamom

Paprika

Dill

Garlic Salt

Onion Powder

Saffron

Coriander

Chinese 5 spice blend

Zaatar spice blend

Baharat spice blend

DAIRY

Full-fat dairy products like yoghurt, butter, heavy **cream,** *and* **sour cream** *are okay in moderation on the* **keto** *diet. But avoid all other milk, low and reduced-fat dairy products.*

Blue cheeses

Blue cheese dressing (recipe included)

Cheddar cheese

Cottage cheese

Cream cheese

Eggs

Ghee

Greek yoghurt

Halloumi

Heavy cream

Mozzarella cheese

Parmesan cheese

Ranch dressing

Ricotta cheese

Sour cream

Unsweetened almond milk

Unsweetened coconut milk

NB: *Fats play a huge part in the ketogenic diet (they make up the majority of your calorie intake),*

so make sure you're taking in plenty of healthy fats.

NUTS

All natural Peanut Butter (2 tbsp = 3.5g net carbs)

Almonds

Brazil nuts

Hazelnuts

Macadamia nuts

Peanuts

Pecans

Pine nuts

Walnuts

SEEDS

Chia seeds

Flaxseeds

Hemp seeds

Pumpkin seeds

Sacha Inca seeds

Sesame seeds

Sunflower seeds

FRUIT

Avocado

Blackberries

Blueberries

Coconut

Cranberries

Lemons

Limes

Raspberries

Strawberries

VEGETABLES

Alfalfa Sprouts

Asparagus

Broccoli

Brussels sprouts

Cabbage

Capsicums

Cauliflower

Celery

Cucumbers

Eggplant

Garlic

Ginger

Green Beans*

Kale

Lettuce

Mushrooms

Olives

Pickles

Pumpkin

Radish

Salad greens

Shallots

Tomato

Zucchini

NB: *Try to stick to green leafy vegetables and avoid root vegetables to keep your daily carbohydrate intake low.*

*Almost all legumes are off limits, but small amounts of green beans are ok.

*Most fruits are off limits on a ketogenic diet. A small amount of berries are considered ok, but watch how much you eat.

SWEETENERS

Following a ketogenic diet involves cutting back on high-carb foods like starches, desserts processed snacks, syrups and sauces. This is essential to reaching a metabolic state called **KETOSIS,** which causes your body to begin breaking down fat stores instead of carbohydrates to produce energy. Ketosis also requires reducing sugar intake, which can make it challenging for those of us with sweet tooths.

Fortunately, there are various low-carb sweets and sweeteners that you can enjoy.

90% Lindt Dark Chocolate

Well Naturally Dark Chocolate Sugar Free Bars

Pure Stevia – is a natural sweetener and in its pure form it contains no carbohydrates.

Erythritol – is a white, powdery sweetener. The structure of its molecules gives it a sweet taste without the side effects of sugar.

ALCOHOL

Believe it or not? There are plenty of low carb alcoholic beverages that you can enjoy in moderation on a Keto-diet. Note, **in moderation** is the key, even low-carb keto-friendly alcohol is full of empty calories, meaning that they supply many calories with little to no central nutrients eg., fibre, vitamins or minerals, and protein.

MIXERS

Mixers are just as important as alcohol itself. When choosing opt for low carb options like diet soft drinks / sodas, sugar-free tonic water, natural mineral waters and soda waters. All of these have 0g carbohydrates keeping your fun-time, Friday night, knock-off work drinks etc., **keto-friendly.**

Alcohol	Serving Size	Carb Content
Gin	45ml / 1.5oz	0g
Rum	45ml / 1.5oz	0g
Tequila	45ml / 1.5oz	0g
Vodka	45ml / 1.5oz	0g
Whiskey	45ml / 1.5oz	0g
Red Wine*	150ml / 5oz	3-4g
White Wine*	150ml / 5oz	3-4g
Light beer	355ml / 12oz	3g

DISCLAIMER: Excessive drinking may also contribute to other serious health conditions including diabetes, heart-disease, liver problems and cancer. For this reason, it's best to keep alcohol intake moderate – defined as 1 drink per day for women and 2 per day for men.

KETO *Unfriendly Foods*

MEAT & MEAT ALTERNATIVES
Deli meat (some, not all)
Hot dogs (frankfurters etc.)
Sausages (with fillers)
Tofu

DAIRY
Almond milk (sweetened)
Coconut milk (sweetened)
Milk
Soy milk
Yoghurt (regular)

NUTS & SEEDS
Cashews
Chestnuts
Pistachios
Seed oils

FRUIT
Apples
Apricots
Bananas
Cherries
Currants
Dates
Grapes
Honeydew melon
Kiwi Fruit
Mangoes
Oranges
Peaches
Pineapples
Plums
Prunes
Rockmelons
Raisins

NB: *As far as fruit and keto go, the main challenge is finding fruits with the lowest sugar and carbohydrate content. Fruits high in sugar — such as apples, bananas, mangos, peaches, and watermelon — are best avoided on the* **keto diet.**

VEGETABLES
Artichokes
Beans
(all varieties except green)
Butternut Squash
Carrots
Chickpeas
Corn
Edamame
Leeks
Parsnips
Peas
Potatoes
Sweet potatoes
Turnips
Water chestnuts

Water

Regardless of diet and lifestyle **WATER** is the MOST important nutrient in our diets.

Drinking water at the correct time of day maximizes its effectiveness on the human body. For optimum health, follow these 4 points.

- 2 glasses of water after waking up helps activate internal organs
- 1 glass 30 minutes before a meal helps digestion
- 1 glass before taking a bath/shower helps lower blood pressure
- 1 glass before going to bed avoids stroke or heart attack

DETOX WATER

- 2 litres (8 cups) of water
- 1 medium cucumber, sliced
- 1 lemon, sliced
- 10 to 12 mint leaves

Combine all ingredients in a large jug and steep overnight in the fridge. Drink every day for general detox and clear skin.

NB: *As a general rule, 1 litre of water per 25kg of weight per day.*

DRINK WATER
SWEAT! EAT WELL! BE HAPPY!

WALKING

Simple, yet incredibly powerful – sneaking in a few extra minutes a day can affect your body, mind and overall health. So, let's get up and get going!

BRAIN: Just 2 hours a week can reduce your risk of stroke by 30%.

MOOD: 30 minutes a day can reduce the symptoms of depression by 36%.

HEALTH: Hitting 3,500 steps per day can lower your risk of diabetes by up to 29%.

MEMORY: 40 minutes 3 times a week protects the memory and planning area of the brain.

LONGEVITY: 75 minutes a week of brisk walking can add around 2 years to your life!

HEART: 30 - 60 minutes most days of the week drastically lowers your risk of heart disease.

WEIGHT: A daily 1 hour walk can cut your risk of obesity by 50%.

BONES: 4 hours a week can reduce the risk of hip fractures by over 40%.

The KETO Plate

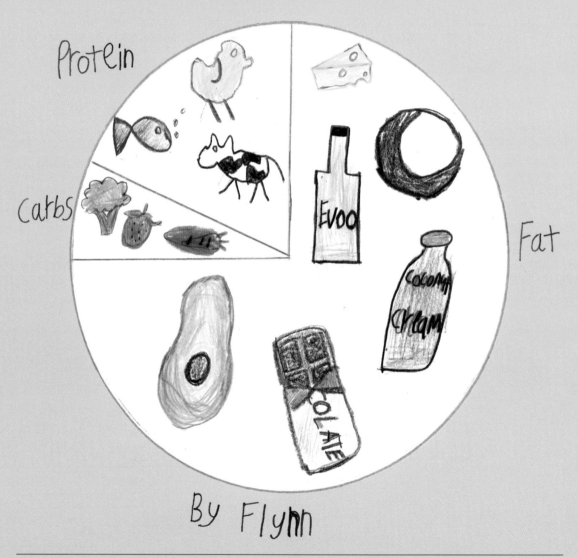

Pie chart adapted from www.higwhheeledmommy.com/2018/04/20/the-not-so-keto-queen.
Drawn by Mr Flynn Turnbull (my 10-year old son).

A Typical Day on the KETO Diet

WATER: It is THE BEST choice for hydration and should be consumed often throughout the day. Adding a little lemon or lime peel, fresh mint or cucumber into your water bottle can make hydration easier for those who struggle.

COFFEE: Black with unsweetened almond milk, or with coconut oil or butter (Bulletproof coffee, also referred to as butter coffee, is popular among clean eating and Paleo devotees too!)

TEA: Unsweetened green tea is delicious and provides many health benefits.

BREAKFAST: A combination of fat plus protein, eggs, cheese, bacon, butter etc.

LUNCH: Grilled chicken, devilled eggs or fresh prawns are fabulous sources of protein. Simply add your favourite salad and be sure to include some heart-healthy avocado, olives, nuts and cheeses.

DINNER: Fish, beef, chicken or pork with cooked vegetables eg., broccoli, mushrooms, pumpkin, zucchini served with avocado, guacamole or whole-egg mayonnaise based sauces.

SNACKS: Hard-boiled eggs, avocado, Keto crackers, nut butter on celery sticks, berries, DIY fat bombs and selected nuts.

Inspiration from KETO DIET: The do's and don'ts of this HFLC nutrition plan www.nola.com/healthy-eating/2017/08/keto_diet_the_dos_and_donts_of

Guide to Weights & Measures

To help a recipe turn out right, you need to measure right.

I have included this simple conversion table to help, regardless of where you are in the world.

Grams – pounds & ounces

Grams (g)	Ounces (oz.)	Grams (g)	Ounces (oz.)
5 g	¼ oz.	225 g	9 oz.
10 g	½ oz.	250 g	10 oz.
25 g	1 oz.	275 g	11 oz.
50 g	2 oz.	300 g	12 oz.
75 g	3 oz.	325 g	13 oz.
100 g	4 oz.	350 g	14 oz.
125 g	5 oz.	375 g	15 oz.
150 g	6 oz.	400 g	1 pound (lb.)
175 g	7 oz.	700 g	1½ lb.
200 g	8 oz.	900 g	2 lb.

Spoons – millilitres (ml)

1 teaspoon	5 ml
1 dessertspoon	10 ml
1 tablespoon	15 ml

Cups – ml – fluid ounces – tablespoons

Cups	ml	Fluid Ounces	Tbsp.
⅛ cup	30 ml	1 fl oz.	2
¼ cup	60 ml	2 fl oz.	4
⅓ cup	80 ml	2.5 fl oz.	5.5
½ cup	125 ml	4 fl oz.	8
⅔ cup	160 ml	5 fl oz.	10.5
¾ cup	190 ml	6 fl oz.	12
1 cup	250 ml	8 fl oz.	16

Table of Contents

What is Keto?   03

Why Keto?   04

Is Keto for me?   05

Keto diets are great and even easy...   06

Keto Friendly Foods   08

Keto Unfriendly Foods   11

Water   12

Walking   13

The Keto Plate   14

A Typical Day on the Keto Diet   15

Guide to Weights & Measures   16

Keto Friendly Breakfasts   18

Keto Friendly Smoothies   42

Keto Friendly Snacks   44

Keto Friendly Dressings   66

Keto Friendly Lunches   68

Keto Friendly Dinners   86

Keto Friendly Sweeties   122

Bibliography   140

Metric Conversion Charts   141

Index   142

KETO FRIENDLY
BREAKFASTS

Nutritional Information

	Per Serve
Calories	115.5
Kilojoules	482.5
Total Fat	4.6g
– Saturated Fat	1.2g
Sodium	76mg
Carbohydrates	5.6g
– Sugar	5.5g
Fibre	3.6g
Protein	8.9g

Baked Eggs in Tomatoes

Serves 2

Tomatoes take on a lovely rich flavour when roasted and can be used in many ways. Use ingredients you have already to create a number of variations. Basil Baked Tomatoes, Parmesan Baked Tomatoes and Pesto Baked Tomatoes are just a few.

- 2 large tomatoes (200g each)
- 1 tablespoon (2g) fresh thyme
- 6 asparagus spears (100g), trimmed
- 2 large eggs (51g each)

Heat the oven to 180°C.

Line a baking tray with baking paper.

Slice the lid off each tomato and use a small spoon to remove the core and seeds, season with sea salt, cracked pepper and thyme.

Place on the prepared baking tray along with the asparagus spears.

Roast for 10 minutes, or until the tomatoes are nice and tender.

Crack an egg into each tomato and lightly season.

Bake for a further 10 minutes or until the eggs are set and cooked to your liking.

Sprinkle with additional thyme leaves to serve.

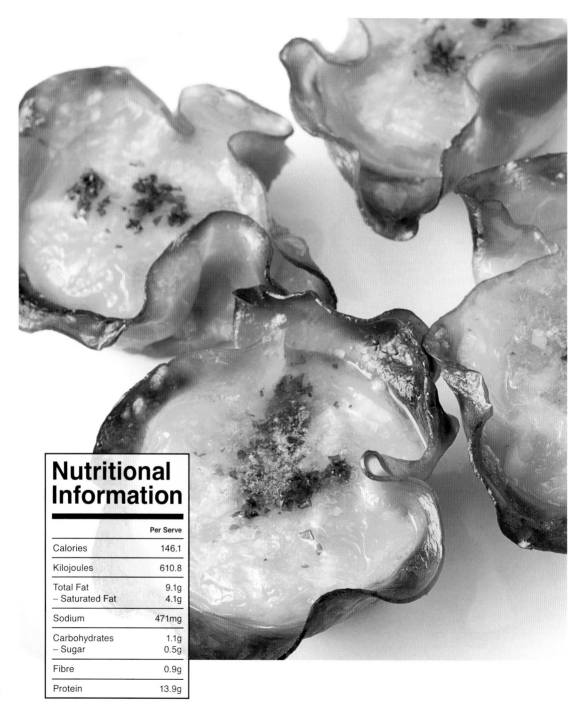

Nutritional Information

	Per Serve
Calories	146.1
Kilojoules	610.8
Total Fat	9.1g
− Saturated Fat	4.1g
Sodium	471mg
Carbohydrates	1.1g
− Sugar	0.5g
Fibre	0.9g
Protein	13.9g

Breakfast Quiches
Makes 8

> "If you look upon Ham & Eggs and lust, you have already committed breakfast in your heart!" — C.S.Lewis

- 8 rounds of fresh ham off the bone (200g)
- 8 large eggs (51g each)
- 1 cup (100g) grated cheddar cheese
- 2 tablespoons (10g) fresh thyme

Preheat oven to 180°C.

Line 8 muffin cups with the rounds of ham.

Crack the eggs into a bowl add three-quarters of the cheese and fresh thyme leaves; season with sea salt and pepper and whisk well.

Divide the egg mixture evenly amongst the cups.

Sprinkle each with remaining cheese and thyme.

Bake for 20 minutes or until golden and set.

Nutritional Information

	Per Serve
Calories	129.5
Kilojoules	541.1
Total Fat	3.4g
– Saturated Fat	1.1g
Sodium	1140.8mg
Carbohydrates	3.5g
– Sugar	2.9g
Fibre	5g
Protein	16.8g

Breakfast STACK
Serves 2

- 4 slices rindless bacon (40g each)
- 2 large field mushrooms (140g each)
- 8 cherry tomatoes (17g each)
- 6 asparagus spears (120g), trimmed

Heat a non-stick frying pan over medium heat and cook the bacon until crispy, 4 to 6 minutes.

Set aside on absorbent paper.

In the same pan, sauté the mushrooms and tomatoes for 2 minutes.

Add the asparagus and season all; cook turning occasionally for 3 to 4 minutes more.

Transfer the mushrooms to a serving plate.

Layer with bacon, asparagus and tomatoes.

OPTIONAL: Serve sprinkled with a little Parmesan Cheese.

FIBRE. PROTEIN. PRODUCE.

Nutritional Information

	Per Serve
Calories	300
Kilojoules	1254.1
Total Fat	22.2g
− Saturated Fat	5.3g
Sodium	1233.7mg
Carbohydrates	2.8g
− Sugar	2.3g
Fibre	4.1g
Protein	20.3g

Classic KETO Breakfast

Serves 2

When I posted this recipe, with this image (shot on my iPhone) to our Instagram page, it went off like a bomb!

- 4 slices rindless bacon (40g each)
- 4 medium eggs (48g each)
- 6 cherry tomatoes (17g each)
- 1 small avocado (180g)

Into a non-stick frying pan over a medium-high heat, cook the bacon until golden brown and crispy, 5 to 6 minutes.

Halfway through, add the tomatoes and sauté.

Remove from pan to absorbent paper.

In a bowl, whisk the eggs vigorously. Whisking not only scrambles eggs, but it adds air and volume for fluffy eggs. Add a splash of water to the eggs and season. The water, when heated on the stove, creates a steaming effect and aids in fluffier eggs; continue to whisk well.

Into the bacon drippings, and over a medium-low heat, pour the egg mixture.

Sit for 1 to 2 minutes, or until the bottom starts to set.

Stir with a spatula, lifting and folding the eggs over themselves.

Let it sit for another 10 seconds then stir and fold again.

Repeat until the eggs are softly set and slightly runny in places.

Remove from the heat and leave for a moment to finish cooking.

Serve on a plate with crispy bacon, sautéed tomatoes and sliced avocado.

Nutritional Information

	Per Serve
Calories	74
Kilojoules	309
Total Fat	5g
– Saturated Fat	1g
Sodium	67mg
Carbohydrates	0g
– Sugar	0g
Fibre	0g
Protein	7g

EASY Boiled Eggs

Makes 2

> "One should not even attend the end of the world without a good breakfast!"
> — Robert A Heinlein

- 2 large eggs (51g each)

Into a medium saucepan, place two eggs.

Fill with cold water, covering them by 2cm.

Bring the water to a gentle, bubbling boil.

The moment the water begins to boil, cover the pan with a lid and cook for 30 seconds.

After 30 seconds, move from heat and sit for 12 minutes for a large egg, 10 minutes for a medium egg.

Remove the eggs and run under cold water to ensure they stop cooking.

Cool completely, about 10 minutes, before peeling.

Store unpeeled eggs in the refrigerator for up to 1 week.

OPTIONAL: For a slightly runny egg, sit for 7 to 8 minutes before running under cold water and slicing off the lid.

Nutritional Information

	Per Serve
Calories	100.3
Kilojoules	419.9
Total Fat	5.4g
– Saturated Fat	1.9g
Sodium	133.3mg
Carbohydrates	3.5g
– Sugar	3.4g
Fibre	1.6g
Protein	8.8g

Eggs 'n' Peppers
Makes 4

> "Today I only eat foods that are life enhancing for me".
> — Louise Hay

- 1 red capsicum (330g)
- 4 medium eggs (48g each)
- 2 tablespoons (20g) grated Parmesan cheese
- 2 tablespoons (10g) fresh coriander leaves

Rinse the capsicum, remove stem and seeds and cut 4 big rings about 1 to 2cm thick.

Warm a non-stick frying pan over low heat, add the rings to the pan and fry on one side for 2 minutes.

Flip and crack an egg into each ring. Season with sea salt and cracked pepper.

Cook for 3 minutes or until cooked the way you like (use a lid and cover if you want them medium or well done).

Remove from heat, use a spatula to place on a serving plate and decorate with fresh coriander or dill.

Nutritional Information

	Per Serve
Calories	171
Kilojoules	715.7
Total Fat	11.8g
– Saturated Fat	5.3g
Sodium	432.4mg
Carbohydrates	0.3g
– Sugar	0.3g
Fibre	0.3g
Protein	15.6g

Herbed Omelette

Makes 2

Rise and Shine! This is a sensational way to start your day.

- 4 medium eggs (48g each)
- 2 tablespoons (10g) flat-leaf parsley
- 2 teaspoons (10g) garlic flavoured olive oil
- ½ cup (50g) freshly shaved Parmesan cheese

In a bowl, combine the eggs and parsley plus 1 tablespoon (30ml) of water.

Season with sea salt and cracked pepper and whisk until frothy.

Heat a 20cm non-stick frying pan over medium heat; add the oil, swirling to coat the base.

Pour in the eggs and sprinkle with Parmesan cheese.

Cook for 2 to 3 minutes, or until the base is set, then lift the omelette over itself and let cook for another 1 to 2 minutes, or until completely set.

Cut in half to serve, sprinkled with a few shavings of Parmesan cheese and fresh herbs.

Nutritional Information

	Per Serve
Calories	463.5
Kilojoules	1937.6
Total Fat	40.4g
– Saturated Fat	9.3g
Sodium	113mg
Carbohydrates	4.3g
– Sugar	3g
Fibre	5.1g
Protein	19.5g

KETO Pancakes
Serves 3

Happiness is... Pancakes for breakfast!

- 1½ cups (150g) almond meal
- 2 tablespoons (4g) stevia
- ½ cup (125ml) coconut milk (or unsweetened milk)
- 2 large eggs (51g each), whisked

In a large bowl mix together almond meal and stevia.

Add coconut milk, eggs and a pinch of salt; using a fork, whisk until just combined (set aside for a few minutes to thicken).

Heat a non-stick frying pan over a medium-low heat and gently pour 3 x quarter cup measures of the mixture into the pan.

Cook until bubbles form on top, 3 to 4 minutes.

Using a long thin spatula, carefully flip and cook the other side for a few minutes more.

Repeat once more, making 6 pancakes.

OPTIONAL: Serve with the delicious Mixed Berry Coulis from P. 125 and a dollop of coconut yoghurt.

Nutritional Information

	Per Serve
Calories	100.3
Kilojoules	419.9
Total Fat	5.4g
– Saturated Fat	1.9g
Sodium	133.3mg
Carbohydrates	3.5g
– Sugar	3.4g
Fibre	1.6g
Protein	8.8g

OMEGA-ME Puddings
Serves 2

Prepare this the night before so it's ready first thing in the morning.
Recipe from *4 Ingredients MORE Gluten Free Lactose Free.*

- 1 cup (250ml) coconut milk
- 2 tablespoons (30g) black chia seeds
- ½ teaspoon (0.25g) stevia

Pour the coconut milk into a bowl,
add black chia seeds and stevia.

Stir well, cover and refrigerate for
at least 1 to 2 hours.

The seeds will plum up, absorbing the liquid,
leaving a delicious 'tapioca-like' pudding.

*OPTIONAL: This super-simple recipe forms
a beautiful base for a number of additions.
Serve it with freshly chopped seasonal fruits,
sprinkled with nuts and berries. Add a
sprinkle of cinnamon, nutmeg or coconut
flakes, raspberries and pistachios... dwell in
the healthy possibilities!*

Nutritional Information

	Per Serve
Calories	237
Kilojoules	988.7
Total Fat	20.6g
– Saturated Fat	15g
Sodium	22.4mg
Carbohydrates	5.7g
– Sugar	4.2g
Fibre	6.9g
Protein	4.4g

Strawberry Chia Pudding
Serves 4

- 400ml coconut milk
- 250g fresh strawberries, washed and hulled
- 4 tablespoons (60g) black chia seeds
- 2 teaspoons (1g) stevia

Purée coconut milk and strawberries in a blender.

Pour into a bowl.

Add chia seeds and stevia.

Whisk well to separate the seeds and combine.

Cover with cling wrap and refrigerate until set, at least 3 to 4 hours.

Stir a couple of times within the first hour to break up any clumps of chia seeds and again just before you are ready to serve.

This pudding is best when fresh, but leftovers will keep covered in the fridge for 2 to 3 days.

Nutritional Information

	Per Serve
Calories	264
Kilojoules	1103.5
Total Fat	22g
– Saturated Fat	9.4g
Sodium	102mg
Carbohydrates	6g
– Sugar	2g
Fibre	3g
Protein	14g

Waffles
Makes 2

- 4 large eggs (51g each)
- ½ cup (155g) almond butter
- 1 tablespoon (2g) stevia
- ½ teaspoon (2g) baking powder

Place all the ingredients in a bowl and beat with an electric hand-mixer, until smooth.

Preheat the waffle machine according to manufacturer instructions.

Once the bubbles in the batter have settled, pour half the batter evenly into the waffle maker and close.

Follow manufacturer instructions to cook, for my machine it took about 3 minutes once heated and the READY sign was on.

Repeat with the remaining batter.

SERVING SUGGESTION: Serve with a simple Berry Coulis P. 125 and a dollop of coconut yoghurt.

WONDERFUL WAFFLES

KETO FRIENDLY SMOOTHIES

Smoothies are a great breakfast or snack that will keep you full for hours.

Here are some of my favourite HFLC smoothie recipes that are ketogenic-friendly and DELICIOUS.

Building a Keto friendly smoothie is easy following these basic guidelines:

1. **Start with a fat-base**
   eg. unsweetened, full-fat coconut milk or a Greek yoghurt made with whole-milk (if you tolerate dairy).

2. **Add some non-starchy veggies**
   eg. spinach, celery, avocados etc.

3. **Include a quality protein source**
   eg. a high-quality protein-powder, egg etc.

4. **Consider a little low-carb fruit**
   eg. blueberries or strawberries.

5. **Add flavour and texture boosters**
   eg. ground cinnamon, ginger, chia seeds etc.

Delicious KETO Iced Coffee

11.5g F
4.4g Carbs

Serves 1
- 2 tablespoons (40g) coconut cream
- ½ cup (125ml) coffee
- ½ cup (125ml) unsweetened almond milk
- ½ teaspoon (4g) cinnamon

Place all the ingredients in a blender with 1½ cups ice cubes and blend until nice and smooth and thick.

OPTIONAL: Add ½ cup chopped cauliflower florets for a thicker consistency – you'll be SURPRISED. This is a low protein breakfast, so to increase that, add 1 teaspoon chia seeds or a scoop of your favourite vanilla-flavoured protein powder.

Strawberry Avocado Smoothie

Serves 1

- 100g frozen strawberries
- ½ cup (125ml) unsweetened almond milk
- ½ avocado (80g)
- 1 teaspoon (0.5g) stevia

Place all ingredients into a blender with 3 ice cubes and blend until smooth. Pour into a glass and enjoy.

20.9g Fat
7.1g Carbs

Green Goddess

20.3g Fat
3.6g Carbs

Serves 1

- 1 handful (30g) English spinach
- 2 baby cukes (40g), chopped
- ½ cup (125ml) coconut milk (from carton)
- 1 teaspoon (0.5g) stevia

Place all ingredients in a blender with 4 ice-cubes
Blend to a smooth consistency.

KETO FRIENDLY
SNACKS

Nutritional Information

	Per Serve
Calories	134.6
Kilojoules	562.6
Total Fat	9.6g
– Saturated Fat	5.3g
Sodium	449.2mg
Carbohydrates	0.5g
– Sugar	0.5g
Fibre	0.7g
Protein	11g

Asparagus Wraps

Serves 8

These are an easy entertainer, a simple finger food that everyone loves.

- 16 asparagus spears (20g each)
- 8 slices of prosciutto (12g each), cut lengthwise
- 200g wheel of camembert cheese, chilled

Preheat oven to 180°C.

Line a baking tray with baking paper.

Trim the asparagus, removing their woody ends.

Bake in the oven for 10 minutes, or until asparagus is tender.

Cut the camembert into 16 thin slices. Take one piece of camembert and wrap it around an asparagus spear. Then tightly wrap one piece of prosciutto around the camembert.

Arrange wrapped spears in a single layer on the prepared tray.

Bake in the oven for an additional 5 minutes.

Season with cracked pepper prior to serving.

Nutritional Information

	Per Serve
Calories	45.5
Kilojoules	190.1
Total Fat	3.7g
– Saturated Fat	1.6g
Sodium	54.8mg
Carbohydrates	0.4g
– Sugar	0.4g
Fibre	0.3g
Protein	2.5g

Caprese Bites
Makes 12

Add some freshness and colour to your next occasion with these tasty bites.

- 12 cherry tomatoes (17g each), halved
- 12 fresh mini-mozzarella balls (120g)
- 12 fresh basil leaves (10g)
- 1 tablespoon (20g) garlic infused olive oil

Onto a toothpick, thread half a tomato, top with a mini mozzarella ball and a fresh basil leaf.

Arrange on a platter.

Drizzle ever so lightly with the garlic infused oil.

Sprinkle with sea salt and cracked pepper.

Serve immediately.

**EASY.
PEASY.
CAPRESE.**

Nutritional Information

	Per Serve
Calories	126
Kilojoules	525.1
Total Fat	9.3g
– Saturated Fat	5.8g
Sodium	144.2mg
Carbohydrates	1g
– Sugar	1g
Fibre	0.4g
Protein	9.4g

Cucumber Tuna Bites

Serves 8

- 2 Lebanese cucumbers (175g each)
- 220g can tuna in brine, drained
- 200g cream cheese
- 1 teaspoon (2g) dill, extra for garnish

Top and tail the cucumbers, either peel or leave as is and cut into 16 even rounds.

Set on a serving board (or plate).

In a bowl, mix together tuna, cream cheese and dill.

Season with cracked pepper and stir to combine.

Spoon (or pipe) the creamy tuna mixture onto the cucumber rounds.

Garnish with fresh dill.

Serve immediately or cover and refrigerate until ready.

OPTIONAL: If you have, add a little lemon zest to the mixture for a lovely fresh flavour.

HOOK
LINE
SINKER

Nutritional Information

	Per Serve
Calories	25.8
Kilojoules	108
Total Fat	1.9g
– Saturated Fat	0.3g
Sodium	46.9mg
Carbohydrates	0.2g
– Sugar	0.1g
Fibre	0.1g
Protein	2g

Devilled Eggs
Makes 12

The term "devilled", in reference to food, was used in the 18th century, the first known print reference appearing in 1786. In the 19th century, it came to be used most often with spicy or zesty food, including eggs prepared with mustard, pepper or other ingredients stuffed in the yolk cavity. They have been a favourite in my family for decades.

- 6 large eggs (51g each)
- 1½ tablespoons (30g) whole-egg mayonnaise
- ½ teaspoon (4g) curry powder
- 1 tablespoon (2g) chopped parsley

Place eggs in a saucepan full of cold water and bring to the boil (this is important to stop them from cracking as they cook).

Once boiling, lower to a simmer and cook for 6 minutes. Pour out the boiling water and cover in cold water to stop them cooking any further (also stops the yolks from discolouring).

Once cold, cut the eggs into 12 halves.

Scoop out the yolks into a small bowl and mix with mayonnaise and curry powder.

Season with sea salt and pepper and add the parsley; stir to combine.

Place a spoon of the yolk mixture back into the egg white.

Arrange the halves onto a plate to serve.

SERVING TIP: Garnish with fresh herbs or a sprinkling of cayenne pepper.

Nutritional Information

	Per Serve
Calories	91.4
Kilojoules	382
Total Fat	7g
– Saturated Fat	3.1g
Sodium	187.2mg
Carbohydrates	4.5g
– Sugar	3.6g
Fibre	0.1g
Protein	2.3g

EASY French Onion Dip

Serves 8

- 1 cup (250ml) Greek yoghurt
- 1 tablespoon (30g) mayonnaise
- 2 tablespoon (20g) dry French onion soup
  (or dehydrated onion flakes)
- 1 teaspoon (6g) Worcestershire sauce

In a mixing bowl, place all the ingredients and season with cracked pepper.

Whisk together until well combined.

Cover and refrigerate for at least 2 hours; allowing plenty of time for the flavours to develop.

Serve chilled.

Optional: This dip is best made in advance and is delicious served with a mezze of fresh vegetable sticks to dip.

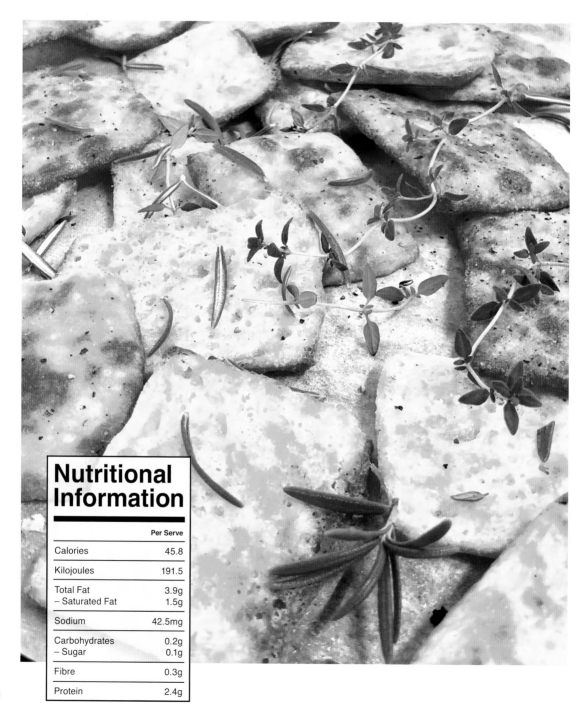

Nutritional Information

	Per Serve
Calories	45.8
Kilojoules	191.5
Total Fat	3.9g
– Saturated Fat	1.5g
Sodium	42.5mg
Carbohydrates	0.2g
– Sugar	0.1g
Fibre	0.3g
Protein	2.4g

KETO Crackers
Makes 32

This recipe was inspired by one we found online from https://kirbiecravings.com/keto-low-carb-crackers/... It's a CRACKER!

- 2 cups (200g) grated mozzarella cheese
- 3 tablespoons (60g) cream cheese
- 1 cup (100g) almond meal
- 1 large egg (51g)

Preheat oven to 180°C.

Line a large baking tray with baking paper.

In a large bowl, add the cheeses, then the almond meal.

Microwave for 30 seconds or until the cheese is just bubbly.

Stir mixture until a smooth dough forms.

Cool for 5 minutes, until just warm to touch.

Add the egg, stir to combine.

Place the dough on top of a sheet of baking paper, place another sheet on top of the dough.

Use a rolling pin to roll out the dough as thinly as possible, 1 to 2mm thick (the thinner the dough, the crispier the cracker).

Use a knife to cut the dough into squares and place on the prepared baking tray.

Bake for 5 minutes, turn and bake for another 5 minutes; or until golden and crispy.

Allow to cool slightly before eating.

Keep uneaten crackers stored in airtight container in fridge.

Reheat in oven to re-crisp crackers.

KETO Grazing Platter

A bright beautiful Keto Grazing Platter is incredibly easy to assemble. I have made many, but the one I love the most goes a little like this...

Onto a platter lay a whole bag of fresh baby spinach or rocket or a mixture of both.

Onto the fresh green add any number of keto-friendly ingredients:

1. **Salami**
   (I twisted the rounds for presentation, they added a little height)
2. **Prosciutto** (as above)
3. **Ham off the bone** (as above)
4. **Truffle cheese**
5. **Brie**
6. **Feta**
7. **Avocado**
8. **Walnuts**
9. **Macadamia Nuts**
10. **Blueberries**
11. **Raspberries**
12. **Baby cukes**
13. **Mini capsicums**
14. **Cherry tomatoes**
15. **Mixed Olives**

A simple substitute for crackers, crostinis, Melba toast etc. are rounds of cucumbers; onto which layer:

- Cream cheese, smoked salmon, capers.

- Cream cheese, smoked salmon, dill.

- A round of cucumber and a square of cheddar cheese.

- **Pepperoni Pizza Bites:**
  A round of pepperoni, a square of cheddar cheese, half a cherry tomato and a fresh basil leaf.

- **Turkey Rollups:**
  A slice of turkey and a slice of Jarlsberg cheese rolled over thinly sliced mini-cukes and red capsicum.

- **Cucumber, Cream Cheese, Salmon Rolls**
  With a vegetable peeler slice the cucumber. Onto a long thin strip, spread cream cheese. Add salmon and sprinkle with fresh dill or capers. Roll to serve.

Nutritional Information

	Per Serve
Calories	45.5
Kilojoules	316.9
Total Fat	5.4g
– Saturated Fat	3.4g
Sodium	243.8mg
Carbohydrates	0g
– Sugar	0g
Fibre	0g
Protein	6.6g

Parmesan Crisps
Makes 12

Float these lovely crisps on top of the Creamy Tomato Soup (P. 71) for dinner, or serve with a pre-dinner drink. But be warned, they are addictive!

– 1 cup (100g) grated Parmesan cheese

Preheat oven to 150°C.

Line a baking tray with baking paper.

Using an egg ring, sprinkle the grated cheese over its base, covering generously.

Remove the egg ring and repeat until cheese is gone.

Bake for 4 to 5 minutes, or until the edges are golden brown, but not burnt.

Remove from oven and cool for 10 minutes.

Serve immediately or store in an air-tight container.

OPTIONAL: Sprinkle with a few fresh thyme leaves before baking.

Nutritional Information

	Per Serve
Calories	15.4
Kilojoules	64.2
Total Fat	0.1g
– Saturated Fat	0.01g
Sodium	451.1mg
Carbohydrates	1.7g
– Sugar	1.7g
Fibre	0.9g
Protein	0.6g

Pink Pickled Onions

Serves 12

Pickled onions sit in my fridge all the time. I use a generous forkful as part of a ploughman's platter, as a healthy snack with a wedge of sharp cheddar cheese, atop steak and have even used the pickle juice as a marinade for pork chops and steak, to tenderise the meat.

- 2 large red onions (180g each), peeled and thinly sliced
- 1 cup (250ml) apple cider vinegar
- 2 teaspoons (12g) sea salt
- 1 teaspoon (3g) black peppercorns

The trick to making pickled onions is to slice the onions very thin, so they soften up and absorb the vinegar resulting in that yummy tangy taste.

Once sliced, place the onions in a large wide-mouth mason jar.

Pour the vinegar over the onions, adding more as needed to cover the top.

Add the salt and peppercorns, seal, and shake the jar vigorously to combine.

Refrigerate for 1 to 2 days before serving.

Nutritional Information

	Per Serve
Calories	45.5
Kilojoules	276.8
Total Fat	4.2g
– Saturated Fat	2.3g
Sodium	175.7mg
Carbohydrates	1g
– Sugar	0.8g
Fibre	0.4g
Protein	5.6g

Ricotta & Prosciutto Baked Pies

Makes 12

- 6 slices prosciutto (80g)
- 400g fresh ricotta
- 6 sprigs (10g) fresh thyme, leaves picked
- 1 bunch chives (20g), coarsely chopped

Preheat oven 180°C.

Line the base and interior of each mini-muffin pan with the prosciutto.

Combine ricotta, thyme and chives in a bowl.

Distribute mixture evenly into muffin section and bake for 15 minutes or until set.

Remove tray and set aside for another 15 minutes to cool before serving.

Optional: Season with sea salt and pepper and bake topped with some halved cherry tomatoes.

EASY.
ELEGANT.
ENTERTAINERS.

2-Ingredient Sauerkraut

0.03g Fat

0.6g Carbs

Serves 8
- 1 head cabbage (200g), thinly sliced
- 1 tablespoon (10g) sea salt

Shred or chop cabbage. Place cabbage into large bowl and add salt. Mash everything with a tamp or your hands to create brine until cabbage is limp and translucent. Pack cabbage and brine tightly into clean container until all of the cabbage is submerged. Ensure cabbage remains submerged by placing a cabbage leaf and a clean weight over the top. Cover with cloth, secure with band. Let sit at room temperature for several days up to 6+ weeks, until it reaches desired flavour. Refrigerate to stop the fermentation process.

Avocado Coriander Lime Mayonnaise

16.2g Fat

0.6g Carbs

Serves 8
- ½ cup (125g) mayonnaise
- 1 medium avocado (160g), pitted
- ¼ cup (20g) chopped coriander
- 2 teaspoons (10ml) lime juice

In a blender, combine the mayonnaise, avocado, coriander and lime juice. Pulse until avocado and mayo are thoroughly combined. Season to taste.

SERVING SUGGESTION: I have served this over grilled salmon and swordfish, dolloped on healthy nachos, and as a dip for fresh veggie sticks.

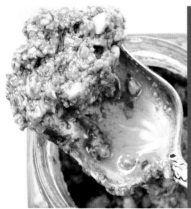

Basil Pesto

40.3g Fat

1.7g Carbs

Serves 6
- 2 cups (25g) fresh basil
- ½ cup (125ml) olive oil
- 1 cup (180g) soaked pine nuts (pistachios or walnuts)
- 6 cloves (18g) garlic, peeled

Combine the basil, olive oil, garlic, and 1 teaspoon sea salt in a high-powered blender. Blend on high until a green basil emulsion forms. Add in nuts and continue blending on high until well combined. Pesto will keep for up to 14 days in the refrigerator.

EASY Blue Cheese Dressing

4.2g Fat
0.5g Carbs

Serves 8
- ⅓ cup (120g) mayonnaise
- ⅓ cup (80g) sour cream
- ⅓ cup (30g) blue cheese
- 1 tablespoon (20ml) fresh lemon juice

Place all ingredients into a blender and season generously with sea salt and cracked pepper. Blend until well combined.

Store in the refrigerator for up to 5 days.

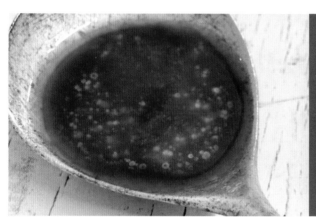

Classic Salad Dressing

12.7g Fat
0.2g Carbs

There are many, but my favourite is:

½ cup (125ml) olive oil +
3 tablespoons (60ml) lemon juice +
1 teaspoon (5g) Dijon mustard.

Season well with sea salt and cracked pepper and shake before serving.

Seafood Sauce

5.8g Fat
3.1g Carbs

Simply mix:

¼ cup (60ml) cream +
2 tablespoons (30g) no added sugar tomato sauce +
a splash of Worcestershire sauce +
a drop of Tabasco sauce.

Season to taste.

KETO FRIENDLY
LUNCHES

Nutritional Information

	Per Serve
Calories	120.1
Kilojoules	718.3
Total Fat	13.7g
– Saturated Fat	5.8g
Sodium	446.9mg
Carbohydrates	8.1g
– Sugar	7.8g
Fibre	3.5g
Protein	2.4g

Creamy Tomato Soup

Serves 4

> "She turned her can'ts into CANS, now she has Tomato Soup."

- 4 tablespoons (80g) unsalted butter
- 1 large onion (165g), peeled and chopped
- 800g can tomatoes, whole peeled or crushed
- 1½ cups (375ml) vegetable stock

In a large saucepan over a medium heat, melt the butter.

Add onion and stir to coat. Season with sea salt and pepper and cook for 1 minute.

Add the tomatoes and stock.

Bring to a gentle boil.

Reduce heat, and simmer, uncovered, for 1 hour.

Stir occasionally.

Cool, before using a hand-held blender to blend until nice and smooth.

RICH.
BOWL.
VELVETY.

Nutritional Information

	Per Serve
Calories	232
Kilojoules	968.1
Total Fat	21g
– Saturated Fat	3.7g
Sodium	344.9mg
Carbohydrates	1.4g
– Sugar	1g
Fibre	1.1g
Protein	9.2g

Egg Caper Salad
Serves 4

- 6 large hard-boiled eggs (51g each), peeled and chopped
- 2 springs onions (15g each), finely chopped
- 2 tablespoons capers (22g), chopped
- ⅓ cup (80g) whole-egg mayonnaise

See hard-boiled egg recipe P. 29.

Once eggs are boiled, peeled and chopped.

Place them and remaining ingredients into a bowl; season with cracked pepper and stir to combine.

OPTIONAL: This is lovely with a little lemon zest added, and served with a fresh garden salad and Keto crackers.

Nutritional Information

	Per Serve
Calories	266.4
Kilojoules	1113.6
Total Fat	19.6g
– Saturated Fat	4.2g
Sodium	485.5mg
Carbohydrates	4g
– Sugar	3.3g
Fibre	2.9g
Protein	17.4g

Prawn Cocktail
Serves 4

These are always popular! Just cut those buttery, delicious avocados in half and fill with the ingredients you use to make a prawn cocktail your family will love.

- 16 large, cooked prawns (300g), peeled and deveined
- 2 medium avocados (280g each)
- 4 lettuce leaves, thinly sliced
- ¼ cup (60g) Seafood Sauce (see P. 67)

Cut the avocados in half and discard the pit.

Scoop half the avocado out, adding the flesh to a bowl, to create a larger round.

Scatter the lettuce evenly across each avocado half and top each with 4 prawns.

Season and mash the avocado.

Spoon across each before serving with a dollop of complimentary seafood sauce.

Nutritional Information

	Per Serve
Calories	189
Kilojoules	790
Total Fat	11.4g
– Saturated Fat	5.3g
Sodium	848.2mg
Carbohydrates	0.4g
– Sugar	0.4g
Fibre	0.1g
Protein	21.1g

Salmon Omelette Rolls
Serves 2

These are delicious and light and can be made ahead of time.

- 4 large eggs (51g each)
- 1 tablespoon (5g) chopped fresh dill
- 2 tablespoons (40g) cream cheese
- 100g sliced smoked salmon

Heat a non-stick pan to medium.

Beat the eggs with chopped dill and season with sea salt and cracked pepper.

Pour half the egg mixture into the heated pan and swirl gently to spread the mixture to the edges of the pan.

Cook for 1 minute or until the base has set.

Carefully flip the omelette and continue to cook for 30-seconds or until golden.

Remove from pan and cool.

Spread each omelette with cream and top with salmon.

Roll up to enclose.

Slice to serve (you may need to secure with a toothpick)..

OPTIONAL: Add finely chopped red onion for flavour and crunch and garnish with extra dill and a wedge of lemon to drizzle.

Nutritional Information

	Per Serve
Calories	562
Kilojoules	2292
Total Fat	45.6g
– Saturated Fat	9.8g
Sodium	1658mg
Carbohydrates	0.9g
– Sugar	0.8g
Fibre	4.9g
Protein	31.8g

Salmon Timbale
Serves 4

- – 4 ripe avocados (180g each)
- – 2 tablespoons (10g) dill, chopped
- – 1 spring onion (10g), finely chopped
- – 500g smoked salmon, chopped

Mash the avocado in a bowl, add the dill and spring onion and season with cracked pepper and a pinch of sea salt.

Place a 6cm timbale (or 3 egg rings stacked atop each other) in the centre of a small serving plate.

Fill with 2 generous tablespoons of avocado mixture and press gently with the back of a spoon.

Add a quarter of the salmon, then 2 more tablespoons of the avocado mixture.

Press gently to compact, and smooth the top.

Carefully remove the timbale and repeat.

NB: These can be assembled up to 30 minutes before serving (just add a teaspoon of fresh lemon juice to the avocado mixture to prevent browning).

OPTIONAL: Serve topped with a selection of fresh microgreens and herbs.

Nutritional Information

	Per Serve
Calories	198.5
Kilojoules	829.6
Total Fat	12g
– Saturated Fat	5.7g
Sodium	533mg
Carbohydrates	1.3g
– Sugar	1.3g
Fibre	7.3g
Protein	17.7g

Spinach & Feta Cakes
Makes 4

- 2 x 250g packets frozen spinach
- ½ cup (60g) marinated feta, drained
- ½ cup (50g) shredded Parmesan, plus more for garnish
- 4 large eggs (51g each), beaten

Into a large bowl, place the spinach and allow time to completely thaw.

In batches, squeeze the excess liquid from it.

Preheat oven to 180°C.

To the spinach add remaining ingredients and season with cracked pepper.

Stir to combine.

Coat 8 cups of a muffin-tray with cooking spray and divide the mixture evenly across each.

Sprinkle with additional Parmesan and bake for 25 to 30 minutes.

Let stand for 5 minutes before serving.

SPINACH & FETA
MATCH MADE IN
HEAVEN

Nutritional Information

	Per Serve
Calories	99.5
Kilojoules	416.1
Total Fat	4.4g
– Saturated Fat	1.2g
Sodium	317.7mg
Carbohydrates	2.2g
– Sugar	0.9g
Fibre	0.8g
Protein	12.3g

Thai Chicken Patties

Makes 8

The secret to successful Thai food is a balance of five flavours; bitter, salty, sour, spicy and sweet. THESE. HAVE. THOSE!

- 500g chicken mince
- 2 shallots (20g), finely chopped
- 1 tablespoon (10g) lime zest
- 2 tablespoons (40g) Gourmet Garden Thai Stir-In Paste

Into a bowl place all the ingredients and season.

Stir to combine well.

Roll into 8 equal size patties.

In a large non-stick frying pan over medium heat, cook the first side for 4 minutes, turn and cook the second side for 4 minutes.

Turn off the heat and sit for 4 minutes.

Serve hot, with sweet chilli sauce, lime wedges, fresh coriander, shredded spring onion and red chilli.

OPTIONAL: When entertaining, make this mixture with pork or chicken, roll into small meatballs and cook. Serve with pre-dinner drinks.

Nutritional Information

	Per Serve
Calories	45.8
Kilojoules	191.4
Total Fat	2g
– Saturated Fat	1.1g
Sodium	158.9mg
Carbohydrates	3.3g
– Sugar	2.5g
Fibre	1.5g
Protein	2.8g

Zucchini Pizzas

Serves 8

These nutritious pizza bites come together in just 10 minutes – Quick. Easy & Delicious!

- 3 zucchini (600g), cut into 2cm rounds
- ⅓ cup (80g) pizza paste
- ½ cup (60g) shredded mozzarella
- 1 tablespoon (10g) Italian seasoning

Preheat oven 180°C.

Heat olive oil in a large frying pan over medium-high heat. Working in batches, add zucchini and cook, flipping once, until golden, about 1 to 2 minutes on each side; season with sea salt and cracked pepper, to taste.

Place zucchini rounds onto a large baking tray.

Top each zucchini round with pizza paste, cheese and Italian seasoning.

Place into oven and cook until the cheese has melted, about 1 to 2 minutes.

Serve immediately, sprinkled with Italian seasoning, or freshly chopped herbs.

KETO FRIENDLY
DINNERS

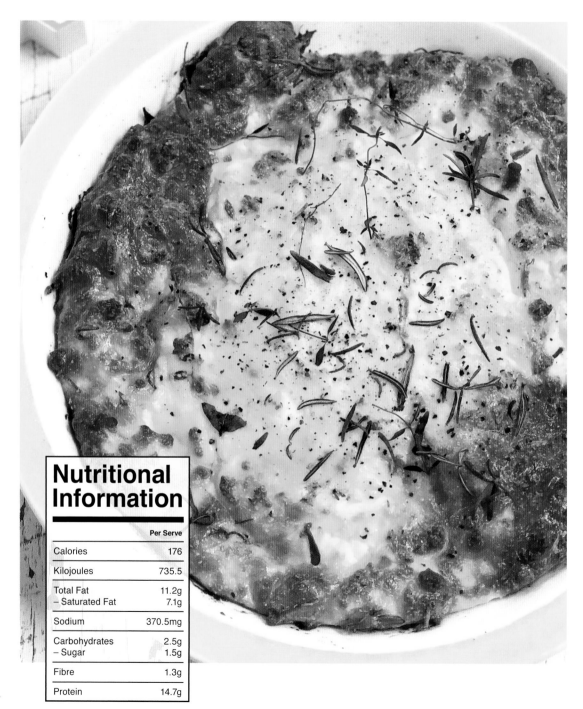

Nutritional Information

	Per Serve
Calories	176
Kilojoules	735.5
Total Fat	11.2g
– Saturated Fat	7.1g
Sodium	370.5mg
Carbohydrates	2.5g
– Sugar	1.5g
Fibre	1.3g
Protein	14.7g

Baked Ricotta Pie

Serves 6

This baked ricotta pie defines easy, elegant, entertaining; it is a creamy, indulgent and crowd-pleasing.

- 425g fresh whole-milk ricotta
- 2 large eggs (51g each)
- 100g Parmesan cheese, grated
- 2 tablespoons (10g) fresh thyme leaves

Preheat the oven to 180°C.

Line a 20cm cake tin with baking paper.

Place all ingredients into a large bowl and season with sea salt and cracked pepper.

Whisk with a fork until well combined.

Pour the mixture to the tin and bake until golden brown, 25 to 30 minutes.

Cool slightly before slicing to serve.

*SERVING SUGGESTION: Serve with a fresh Garden Salad dressed with this simple **Lemon Dressing:** Traditionally, vinaigrettes are made with a 3:1 ratio of oil/acid (eg. 1 cup olive oil, ⅓ cup vinegar); however, sometimes I find that too oily. Here I use a 1:1 ratio and find the balance much better.*

Place ¼ cup each of fresh lemon juice (roughly 2 lemons) and EVOO + 2 teaspoons Dijon mustard into a jar. Season with ¼ teaspoon sea salt and ⅛ teaspoon cracked pepper and shake well. Refrigerate for up to one week; shake before using.

Nutritional Information

	Per Serve
Calories	209.5
Kilojoules	879
Total Fat	11.3g
– Saturated Fat	2.7g
Sodium	367.5mg
Carbohydrates	10.4g
– Sugar	8.8g
Fibre	3.7g
Protein	13.9g

Basil Pesto Frittata

Serves 4

Frittata, which translates to "fried" in Italian, is an egg-based classic brunch dish. It is similar to an omelette, crustless quiche, and Spanish tortilla and is a great way to use up leftover dips, pestos and vegetables.

- 200g pumpkin, peeled and diced into 1cm cubes
- ½ cup (60g) red capsicum, deseeded and diced
- 2 tablespoons (40g) basil pesto
- 4 large eggs (51g each), lightly beaten

Preheat oven to 180°C.

Line a baking tray with baking paper.

Spread the pumpkin and capsicum evenly, and spray lightly with olive oil.

Roast for 20 minutes or until golden brown and tender.

Transfer to a non-stick, 20cm frying pan.

In a separate bowl, combine the pesto and eggs, then pour over the roasted vegetables.

Over a medium-low heat, cook for 8 minutes.

Return to the oven for 5 minutes to set.

Using oven mitts, carefully remove to a serving plate.

Nutritional Information

	Per Serve
Calories	299.5
Kilojoules	1252
Total Fat	13.6g
– Saturated Fat	6.1g
Sodium	293.8mg
Carbohydrates	0.7g
– Sugar	0.7g
Fibre	1.1g
Protein	42.8g

Blue Cheese Pork with Asparagus

Serves 6

This recipe is truly dinner party worthy, it is the epicentre of pork deliciousness (if there is such a thing?)

- 4 thick pork chops (200g each)
- ½ cup (50g) crumbled blue cheese
- 2 teaspoons (10g) butter
- 12 asparagus spears (200g)

Cut a horizontal slit through the thickest portion of each pork cutlet, and gently twist to form a pocket.

Stuff 2 teaspoons of crumbled blue cheese into each.

Season both sides with sea salt and cracked pepper.

In a large non-stick frying pan, cook the pork for 3 to 4 minutes each side, or until cooked through but still juicy.

Remove the pork from the pan, cover with foil and rest for 5 minutes.

Add the butter to the pan, swirl to melt and coat the base.

Add the asparagus spears, season and cook, turning occasionally, until lightly browned, about 3 minutes.

Serve the pork with the sautéed asparagus.

Nutritional Information

	Per Serve
Calories	167
Kilojoules	698
Total Fat	4.1g
– Saturated Fat	0.8g
Sodium	296.8mg
Carbohydrates	8.7g
– Sugar	3.3g
Fibre	2.3g
Protein	25.6g

Chicken, Mushroom & Pesto Stack
Serves 4

DID YOU KNOW 62% of Australians eat chicken twice a week? Here's another to add to your repertoire.

- 4 medium, skinless chicken breast halves (150g each)
- 4 medium field mushrooms (150g each)
- 4 tablespoons (80g) basil pesto
- 4 small tomatoes (100g each)

Preheat oven to 180°C.

Place field mushrooms and tomatoes in an oven dish and drizzle with a little oil (optional). Season with sea salt and cracked pepper. Roast for 20 minutes.

Heat a non-stick frying pan or grill over a medium-high heat, season chicken breasts before grilling 6 minutes, flip and grill for another 6 minutes or until cooked through. Set aside.

Spoon pesto into a small microwave dish and warm for 30 seconds, stir to distribute the heat.

To serve place a mushroom on each plate, top with chicken, a tablespoon of pesto and a roasted tomato.

EAT YOURSELF HEALTHY

Nutritional Information

	Per Serve
Calories	267.8
Kilojoules	1119.3
Total Fat	15.5g
– Saturated Fat	7g
Sodium	357mg
Carbohydrates	0.1g
– Sugar	0.1g
Fibre	0.3g
Protein	31.6g

Greek Lamb Meatballs

Serves 4

- 500g lamb mince
- 1 large egg (51g)
- 2 teaspoons (10g) lemon zest
- 100g feta, crumbled

Into a large bowl, add all the ingredients (this is optional, but if you have, add a clove of garlic, crushed and some freshly chopped parsley) .

Season with cracked pepper and stir to combine.

Roll tablespoons of mixture into balls (damp hands will help).

Place on a plate.

In a large frying pan over a medium-high heat, cook the meatballs, turning, for 6 to 7 minutes, or until browned and cooked through.

Serve with a fresh Greek salad.

*OPTIONAL: Serve with this fabulous **Keto Tzatziki:** Into a bowl, place 2 baby cukes (25g each) that have been diced, 300g natural coconut yoghurt, 1 clove garlic, crushed and 1 tablespoon finely chopped fresh dill. Season with sea salt and cracked pepper and add a little lemon zest if you have it. Stir to combine. Serve immediately or cover and store in the refrigerator for up to 5 days.*

7.9g Fat
1.3g Carbs

Nutritional Information

	Per Serve
Calories	362
Kilojoules	1515.8
Total Fat	20.2g
– Saturated Fat	15.4g
Sodium	723mg
Carbohydrates	3.5g
– Sugar	2.6g
Fibre	1.0g
Protein	41.3g

Green Chicken Curry
Serves 4

This recipe is from a cookbook I wrote called 4 Ingredients MORE Gluten Free Lactose Free. It is endorsed by Coeliac Australia and is a cookbook for anyone wanting to be healthier following a gluten and lactose free diet.

- 3 tablespoons (84g) green curry paste
- 2 teaspoons (12g) fish sauce
- 400ml coconut milk
- 700g skinless chicken breast, diced

Heat a large non-stick frying pan over a medium heat.

Add the chicken and sauté for 3 to 4 minutes or until just golden.

Add the curry paste and fish sauce and toss to coat the chicken.

Reduce the heat, and add the coconut milk.

Simmer for 10 minutes, stirring occasionally, until cooked.

Season to taste.

OPTIONAL: This is a fabulous veggie smuggling recipe. Add all sorts of seasonal vegetables, in particular green beans, snow peas and strips of red capsicum, carrots and zucchini. Similarly, stir through some bamboo shoots right at the end so they are warm, but retain their crunchiness. I serve this with rice for my boys ½ cup (100g) cooked Jasmine rice (187 calories) and over fresh English spinach for my husband and I. Garnish with greens to serve.

Nutritional Information

	Per Serve
Calories	296
Kilojoules	1236.5
Total Fat	17.2g
– Saturated Fat	2.6g
Sodium	198.3mg
Carbohydrates	2.4g
– Sugar	2.4g
Fibre	0.8g
Protein	31.9g

Grilled Fish with Tartare Sauce
Serves 4

- 4 white fish fillets (200g each)
- 1 tablespoon (20ml) olive oil
- 1 lemon, cut into wedges
- 4 tablespoons (80g) tartare sauce

Oil the fish and season lightly.

Heat a non-stick frying pan over a medium-high heat.

When hot, add the fish and cook for 2 to 3 minutes or until golden, gently flip and cook the underside, 2 minutes or until cooked through.

Transfer each to a plate.

Season with cracked pepper, a splash of fresh lemon juice, a wedge of lemon and a good dollop of tartare sauce.

SERVING SUGGESTION: Serve with fresh garden greens.

Nutritional Information

	Per Serve
Calories	148.5
Kilojoules	621.8
Total Fat	5.9g
– Saturated Fat	2g
Sodium	60.8mg
Carbohydrates	1.1g
– Sugar	0.8g
Fibre	0.6g
Protein	22.1g

Mediterranean Rosemary Skewers

Serves 4

This recipe is from 4 Ingredients MORE Gluten Free Lactose Free and is a family favourite of ours. It's just so versatile, you can substitute chicken or beef for lamb and add any number of fresh vegetables. As you can see from the photo, we added Kalamata olives, cherry tomatoes and rolled zucchini. A button mushroom would be a great companion too.

- 8 fresh rosemary stalks (20cm long)
- 4 medium lamb chops (180g each)
- 4 cloves garlic (12g), crushed
- 3 tablespoons (60ml) fresh lemon juice and zest

Remove the bottom two-thirds of rosemary leaves from each stalk and cut a sharp point into the end.

Cut the lamb into chunks, then in a large bowl, combine lamb, garlic, lemon juice and zest with 2 tablespoons chopped rosemary leaves.

Season with cracked pepper, cover with cling wrap and marinade for at least 2 hours.

Thread onto rosemary skewers, adding whatever vegetables you like.

Grill over a medium-high heat for 8 to 10 minutes turning occasionally until cooked to desired tenderness.

Baste with marinade throughout.

Nutritional Information

	Per Serve
Calories	250.6
Kilojoules	1047.4
Total Fat	6.5g
– Saturated Fat	2.3g
Sodium	359.8mg
Carbohydrates	12.6g
– Sugar	11.6g
Fibre	5.1g
Protein	32.8g

Mediterranean Stuffed Capsicums
Serves 4

DID YOU KNOW? Green capsicums are unripe, yellow riper and red the ripest of all. Stuffing a red capsicum and baking it results in a naturally sweet and lovely case and is much better for you than the usual pastry cases made of carb-dense dough.

- 2 red capsicums (260g each), cut in half lengthways (membranes and seeds discarded)
- 1 large onion (180g), peeled and chopped
- 500g lean beef mince
- 1 cup (250ml) Pasta sauce

Heat a little olive oil in large non-stick frying pan, add onion; cook, stirring, until tender.

Add beef and cook, stirring, until browned.

Add pasta sauce, bring to a gentle boil.

Reduce heat; simmer, uncovered, 10 minutes, stirring occasionally, season to taste.

Meanwhile, line a baking dish with baking paper. Lay the 4 capsicum halves inside.

Fill each with the mince mixture. Bake, uncovered, for 40 minutes or until capsicums are tender.

OPTIONAL: this is a great veggie smuggling recipes. Add extra veggies to the mince, such as diced celery, zucchini, garlic and parsley and before baking sprinkle with a little Parmesan cheese.

Nutritional Information

	Per Serve
Calories	151.6
Kilojoules	633.7
Total Fat	8.2g
– Saturated Fat	5.1g
Sodium	322.2mg
Carbohydrates	3.2g
– Sugar	3.1g
Fibre	0.3g
Protein	16.2g

Prawns with Creamy Dipping Sauce

Serves 6

- ½ cup (125ml) cream
- ¼ cup (60ml) no added sugar tomato sauce
- 1 tablespoon (20ml) fresh lemon juice
- 24 large cooked prawns (450g), peeled (leaving tails intact)

To make the cocktail sauce, combine the cream, tomato sauce and lemon juice in a small bowl.

Season to taste (you can add a splash of Worcestershire sauce and Tabasco if you have them, depending on how spicy you like your Seafood Sauce?) and pour into a little ramekin.

Fill a large, round serving bowl three-quarters with ice.

Drape the prawns around its lip and over the ice.

Into the dish, place the Seafood Sauce.

Garnish with wedges of lemon and serve immediately.

Nutritional Information

	Per Serve
Calories	433.9
Kilojoules	1813.7
Total Fat	26g
– Saturated Fat	5.6g
Sodium	825.8mg
Carbohydrates	1.9g
– Sugar	1.6g
Fibre	1.8g
Protein	47.1g

Salmon BLT
Serves 4

This recipe is truly dinner party worthy.

- 4 slices (200g) bacon, chopped
- 4 salmon steaks (198g each), skinless
- 12 cherry tomatoes (17g each)
- 60g English spinach

Cook the bacon over medium heat in a large non-stick frying pan until crispy.

Remove and set aside.

Add the salmon fillets and season with sea salt and cracked pepper, cook for 3 minutes each side.

Serve each fillet on a plate, topped with spinach, crispy bacon and sautéed tomatoes.

Optional: Serve with a dollop of homemade **Lemon Mayonnaise:** *Mix together ¼ cup (80g) mayonnaise, juice and zest of ½ a lemon and ¼ teaspoon cayenne pepper ~ YUM!*

FRESH. JUICY. TENDER.

Nutritional Information

	Per Serve
Calories	419
Kilojoules	1750.2
Total Fat	25.2g
– Saturated Fat	4.6g
Sodium	196.3mg
Carbohydrates	9.7g
– Sugar	6.7g
Fibre	4g
Protein	36.4g

Salmon Pesto Salad

Serves 4

Whip up this deliciously easy meal for the family. The pesto and spinach pair perfectly with the salmon.

- 500g butternut pumpkin,
  peeled and cut into even 4cm x 4cm chunks
- 4 x 150g salmon fillets
- 150g English spinach
- 2 tablespoons (40g) basil pesto

Preheat oven 180°C.

Place the pumpkin on a baking tray and season with sea salt and cracked pepper.

Cook for 15 minutes or until tender.

After 5 minutes, place the salmon fillets on another baking tray, season with cracked pepper and bake for 10 minutes.

Remove both, place the cooked pumpkin into a large bowl, add the spinach and pesto and toss to combine.

To serve, place the delectable salad on a plate and nestle a salmon fillet amongst it.

Nutritional Information

	Per Serve
Calories	110
Kilojoules	459.9
Total Fat	5.4g
– Saturated Fat	2g
Sodium	341.4mg
Carbohydrates	4.5g
– Sugar	3.8g
Fibre	0.9g
Protein	10.5g

San Choi Bau

Serves 4

- 500g pork mince
- 4 tablespoons (80g) hoisin sauce
- 1 small red capsicum (160g)
- 12 cos lettuce leaves (10g each)

In a non-stick frying pan over a medium heat, cook the mince.

Use a wooden spoon to separate and cook until browned.

Add the capsicum, season with cracked pepper and stir to combine.

Add the hoisin sauce, reduce heat and simmer for 10 to 12 minutes.

Remove from heat to cool slightly.

Carefully remove lettuce leaves so they remain intact and trim into round, dish-like bowls, and place on a platter.

Spoon the tasty pork mixture evenly across the lettuce cups.

Serve immediately garnished with freshly diced capsicum.

Optional: These are a fabulous veggie smuggler so grate in or add in whatever vegetables you have and serve with a fresh wedge of lime to squeeze over.

Nutritional Information

	Per Serve
Calories	433.9
Kilojoules	560.6
Total Fat	9.2g
– Saturated Fat	4.7g
Sodium	56.9mg
Carbohydrates	1.2g
– Sugar	0.8g
Fibre	0.5g
Protein	11.7g

Satay Pork Skewers
Makes 8

My how we love satay. Satay is a dish with its origins in Indonesia and Malaysia consisting of small pieces of meat grilled on a skewer and served with a spiced sauce that typically contains peanuts. Sweet. Salty. Satay.

- ¾ cup (185mL) coconut milk
- 2 tablespoons (50g) crunchy peanut butter
- 1 teaspoon (8g) curry powder
  (depending on how spicy you like it, add more)
- 2 pork chops (200g each), trimmed and cut into 2cm cubes

In a medium bowl, mix together the coconut milk, peanut butter, curry powder and season with sea salt and cracked pepper.

Add the pork, stir to coat, marinate for at least 1 hour in the refrigerator.

When ready to cook, thread the pork onto metal skewers (or bamboo skewers pre-soaked).

Grill, turning every minute so as not to burn, 4 to 5 minutes or until cooked.

Continue to glaze throughout.

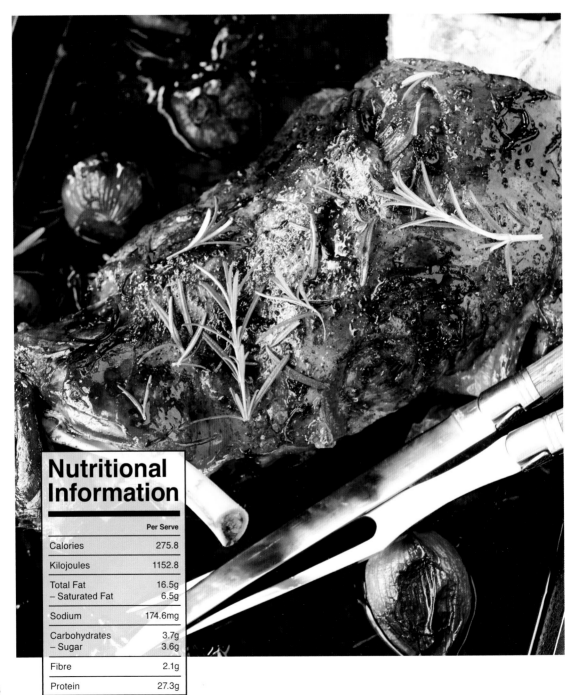

Nutritional Information

	Per Serve
Calories	275.8
Kilojoules	1152.8
Total Fat	16.5g
– Saturated Fat	6.5g
Sodium	174.6mg
Carbohydrates	3.7g
– Sugar	3.6g
Fibre	2.1g
Protein	27.3g

Slow Cooked Lamb with Onions & Rosemary

Serves 8

A dependable Sunday family dinner that I serve with roasted broccoli, mushrooms, pumpkin and zucchini.

- 2kg lamb shoulder bone-in
- 6 little brown onions (50g each), peeled
- 6 rosemary sprigs (3g each)
- 1 cup (250mL) chicken stock

In a large frying pan over a high heat, brown the shoulder on all sides, 2 minutes each side. Then transfer to slow cooker.

Season heavily with sea salt and cracked pepper.

Remove the leaves from rosemary sprigs and scatter around the lamb.

Add the onions and chicken stock.

Cover and cook on low for 6 to 8 hours, at which point, the lamb should be so tender that all you need to do is tear the meat away with tongs.

Serve the lamb on a platter with the onions and drizzle with delicious melty onion sauce.

SUNDAY ROASTS ARE A TRADITION WORTH SAVING

Nutritional Information

	Per Serve
Calories	600
Kilojoules	2506.9
Total Fat	44g
– Saturated Fat	21g
Sodium	132.4mg
Carbohydrates	1.6g
– Sugar	1.6g
Fibre	0.8g
Protein	49.1g

Steak with Creamy Mushroom Sauce

Serves 2

While the steaks are resting, make your own simple sauce using the pan juices and a couple extra ingredients. This is a luxurious, yet simple sauce you will make over and over again.

- 2 x 200g scotch fillet or steak of your choice
- 1 tablespoon (20ml) olive oil
- 1 cup (120g) button mushrooms, sliced
- ½ cup (125ml) cream

Heat a non-stick frying pan to high.

Brush the steaks with oil. Season with sea salt and cracked pepper.

Cook the first sides of the steaks until moisture appears (approx. 4 minutes), turn and cook for another 4 minutes for medium doneness.

Remove from the pan, cover with foil, and allow to rest.

Into the same pan, add the mushrooms, stirring to blend with the pan juices.

Add the cream and stir again until well combined.

Lower heat and simmer to reduce and thicken slightly.

Serve each steak with the decadent mushroom sauce.

Nutritional Information

	Per Serve
Calories	314.5
Kilojoules	1313.3
Total Fat	19.9g
– Saturated Fat	7.6g
Sodium	680.3mg
Carbohydrates	5.7g
– Sugar	4.4g
Fibre	2.1g
Protein	26.3g

Texan Pork Chops
Serves 2

- 2 pork loin chops (150g each), 2cm thick
- 1 cup (175g) salsa
- 12 jalapenos (12g), chopped

In a large non-stick frying pan, cook seasoned pork for 5 minutes or until golden.

Turn once, cook for a further 4 to 5 minutes or until golden and done.

Remove and set aside to rest.

Into the pan, add the salsa and scatter with jalapenos.

Reduce the heat to medium and cook for 5 minutes, stirring often.

Dollop the deliciously spicy salsa onto a plate and top with a chop...

What could be simpler?

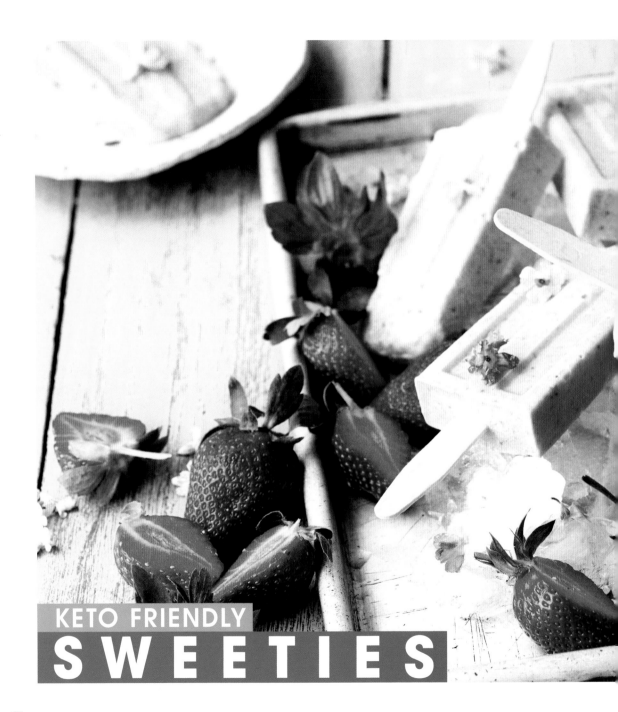

KETO FRIENDLY
SWEETIES

Nutritional Information

	Per Serve
Calories	202.7
Kilojoules	847.5
Total Fat	18g
– Saturated Fat	9.6g
Sodium	5.3mg
Carbohydrates	6.1g
– Sugar	5.7g
Fibre	3.1g
Protein	3.2g

Berry Parfaits
Serves 2

- 1 cup (255g) frozen mixed berries
- 1 teaspoon (0.5g) stevia
- ½ cup (125g) coconut yoghurt
- 2 tablespoons (20g) walnuts, chopped

In a small saucepan, place the berries.

Add 1 tablespoon (20ml) water, stevia and a pinch of salt and bring to a gentle boil.

Reduce the heat and simmer for 10 minutes, the berries will begin to break down and the sauce thicken slightly.

Cool before building the parfaits.

Into 2 serving cups divide the berry coulis.

Top with yoghurt and sprinkle with walnuts.

OPTIONAL: You can literally make a Coulis from any berry. Coulis is a fancy French way to say sauce, it's a thin puree of fruit reduced down with a sweetener. Use the same quantities and method to make Blackberry Coulis, Raspberry Coulis or even Strawberry Raspberry Coulis, each of these will brighten many a Sweet Treat.

Nutritional Information

	Per Serve
Calories	113.3
Kilojoules	473.4
Total Fat	9.7g
– Saturated Fat	4.5g
Sodium	36mg
Carbohydrates	3.7g
– Sugar	2.3g
Fibre	0.6g
Protein	2.9g

Cheesecake KETO Bombs
Makes 12

125g cream cheese

¼ cup (80g) natural peanut butter

1 tablespoon (2g) stevia

80g dark chocolate, grated (60%+)

In a bowl, combine cream cheese, peanut butter and stevia.

Stir until well combined.

Chill for 10 minutes.

Using a teaspoon and damp hands; roll into small balls.

Gently sprinkle and roll into grated chocolate to coat.

Refrigerate to set.

Nutritional Information

	Per Serve
Calories	211.8
Kilojoules	885.5
Total Fat	21.3g
– Saturated Fat	11.3g
Sodium	11mg
Carbohydrates	2.7g
– Sugar	2.4g
Fibre	2.4g
Protein	1.8g

CocoAvo Ice-cream Cake
Serves 6

2 avocados (180g each)

400ml coconut cream

1 tablespoon (2g) stevia

50g fresh mixed berries (strawberries, blueberries, raspberries) + edible flowers

Cut the avocados in half and discard the pit.

Scoop the avocado out, adding the flesh to a food processor.

Add the coconut cream and 1 tablespoon stevia.

Season with a pinch of salt and purée until nice and smooth.

Taste to determine if you need more stevia.

Pour into a paper-lined loaf tin, cover with cling wrap and freeze for 3 to 4 hours or until set.

Serve on a long, rectangular platter garnished with fresh berries and edible flowers.

Nutritional Information

	Per Serve
Calories	298
Kilojoules	1245.1
Total Fat	30.1g
– Saturated Fat	22g
Sodium	8mg
Carbohydrates	3.6g
– Sugar	3.1g
Fibre	1.5g
Protein	3.7g

Coconut Yoghurt with Walnuts & Spices

Makes 1

150g coconut yoghurt

4 walnuts (8g), chopped

¼ teaspoon (0.7g) ground cinnamon

¼ teaspoon (0.7g) ground nutmeg

This is not much of a recipe, but a reminder of how popular a simple bowl of good, wholesome yoghurt can be as a light, lovely dessert.

One of my favourites, simply stir all the ingredients together and spoon into a serving bowl.

Serve sprinkled with a little extra ground cinnamon.

OPTIONAL: Stir through 6 frozen blueberries for a pretty purple hue.

Nutritional Information

	Per Serve
Calories	168.5
Kilojoules	704.2
Total Fat	12.8g
– Saturated Fat	8.2g
Sodium	34.5mg
Carbohydrates	9.4g
– Sugar	9.2g
Fibre	1.9g
Protein	2.9g

Cinnamon Dip

Serves 4

250g light sour cream

1 tablespoon (15g) ground cinnamon

2 teaspoons (1g) stevia

250g fresh strawberries, washed

In a bowl, mix together sour cream, cinnamon and stevia.

Cover with cling wrap and refrigerate for 1 hour, allowing time for the flavours to meld together.

When ready to serve, spoon the cream into a pretty serving bowl; place it on a platter surrounded by fresh, ripe, red strawberries.

OPTIONAL: You could use a regular fat sour cream, but I find the light sour cream a nicer dip consistency, not quite as thick. Doing this would almost double the fat content and reduce the carbohydrate content by 10 - 15%.

Nutritional Information

	Per Serve
Calories	86.1
Kilojoules	359.9
Total Fat	6.8g
– Saturated Fat	3.2g
Sodium	9.8mg
Carbohydrates	4.9g
– Sugar	2.9g
Fibre	0.9g
Protein	1.2g

ChocCado Truffles

Makes 12

1 cup (175g) dark chocolate, grated (60%+)

1 medium avocado (160g)

1 teaspoon (5g) vanilla extract

¼ cup (25g) raw cacao powder

In a medium bowl, combine melted chocolate with avocado and vanilla.

Season with sea salt (optional) and stir together until nice and smooth.

Refrigerate for 20 minutes.

Sprinkle the cacao powder onto a plate.

With slightly dampened hands, use a heaped teaspoon of mixture and roll into balls.

Roll in cocoa powder.

Refrigerate in an airtight container.

Nutritional Information

	Per Serve
Calories	51.7
Kilojoules	216.2
Total Fat	4.9g
– Saturated Fat	2.5g
Sodium	33.6mg
Carbohydrates	0.5g
– Sugar	0.3g
Fibre	0.3g
Protein	1.4g

Pistachio Crusted Truffles
Makes 12

1 cup (250g) cream cheese

1 teaspoon (0.5g) stevia

½ teaspoon (0.5g) ground cinnamon

¼ cup (30g) pistachios, crushed

In a small bowl, combine cream cheese, stevia and cinnamon.

Mix well to combine.

Chill for 30 minutes.

Roll by hand into 12 balls, about 2cm in diameter
(NB: If too soft to roll, chill for 10 minutes and try again).

Place the pistachios on a small plate and roll the truffles in them until completely coated.

Chill 30 minutes before serving.

Store in an airtight container in the refrigerator for up to one week or in the freezer for up to 3 months.

Nutritional Information

	Per Serve
Calories	191
Kilojoules	797.3
Total Fat	18.3g
– Saturated Fat	10.4g
Sodium	83.9mg
Carbohydrates	2.6g
– Sugar	1.5g
Fibre	1.2g
Protein	3.9g

Frozen Fat Bombs

Makes 18

- ¾ cup (185g) coconut oil
- 1 cup (312g) peanut butter
- 1 tablespoon (7g) cacao powder
- 1 tablespoon (2g) stevia

Into a microwaveable jug place the coconut oil and peanut butter and microwave in 30-second increments, stirring after each until nice and smooth.

Add the cacao powder and stevia and mix thoroughly.

Pour across 18 ice-cube moulds.

Freeze for at least 4 hours or until set.

Nutritional Information

	Per Serve
Calories	90.3
Kilojoules	377.3
Total Fat	8.2g
– Saturated Fat	6.7g
Sodium	7.7mg
Carbohydrates	2.7g
– Sugar	2.4g
Fibre	1.5g
Protein	1g

Strawberry Fields Forever
Makes 10

You can't buy happiness, but you can make ice-cream and they are kind of the same thing at the end of the day!

- 400ml coconut cream
- 250g strawberries, washed, hulled, chopped
- 1 tablespoon (2g) stevia
- 1 tablespoon (15g) black chia seeds

Add all the ingredients to a blender.

Blend until smooth, scraping down the sides of the blender as needed.

Season to taste (may need a little more sweetener).

Pour into ⅓ cup capacity ice-block moulds and insert a stick in the end.

Freeze for at least 4 to 6 hours, or overnight.

Enjoy immediately.

OPTIONAL: To increase the protein content, add 1 tablespoon of your favourite vanilla protein powder before blending.

SWEETS 4 KETOTARIANS

Shortbread Cookies

Makes 18

12g Fat
3.3g Carbs

- 6 tablespoons (90g) salted butter
- ½ cup (100g) 100% Natural Sweetener
- 1 teaspoon (2g) vanilla extract
- 2½ cups (160g) almond meal

Preheat the oven 180°C. Line a baking tray with baking paper.

Use a hand mixer to beat together the butter and stevia, until it's fluffy and light in colour. Beat in the vanilla extract (if you don't have salted butter, add a pinch of salt).

Beat in the almond meal, half a cup at a time.
NB: The dough should stick when pressed together.

Scoop rounded tablespoonfuls of the dough onto the prepared tray.
Flatten each cookie with the back of a spoon to about half-1cm thick (you can make them as thick or thin as you like, they will be crispier if thinner).

Bake for 12 minutes, or until the edges are golden.
Allow to cool completely in the pan before handling (cookies will harden a little as they cool).

OPTIONAL: I added a teaspoon of lemon zest when adding the butter mixture to the almond meal for a lovely fresh flavour. If entertaining, or giving as a gift, I would drizzle with dark chocolate.

Strawberry & PB Fudge

Makes 8

- ½ cup (100g) diced strawberries
- 2 teaspoons (1g) stevia
- ½ cup (160g) peanut butter
- 2½ tablespoons (50g) coconut oil

Purée the strawberries. Add the stevia and stir. Set aside. In a microwave-safe bowl, place the peanut butter and coconut and microwave for 30 seconds or until nice and smooth. Cool for 5 minutes. Stir in the strawberry mixture, until well combined. Pour mixture into 8 ice cube moulds and freeze to set, 2 to 3 hours.

10.8g Fat
3.5g Carbs

Nuts About These

"Sometimes it's the smallest things that satisfy the greatest cravings"

1.2g Fat
0.3g Carbs

Makes 40

- 100g dark chocolate, broken (60%+)
- 40 pecan halves

Line a baking tray with baking paper. In a microwaveable bowl, melt the chocolate in 30-second increments stirring after each, until smooth and creamy. Dip the pecans, completely coating some, and only partially coating others. Place on the prepared tray and, when finished, refrigerate to set.

TAKE CARE OF YOUR BODY.
IT'S THE ONLY PLACE YOU HAVE TO LIVE IN.

Please Join Us

---

4 Ingredients is a family of busy people bound together by the desire to create good, healthy, homemade meals quickly, easily and economically.

Our aim is to save us all precious time and money in the kitchen. If this is you too, then we invite you to join our growing family where we share kitchen wisdom daily.

Similarly, if you have a favourite recipe or a tip that has worked for you in the kitchen and think others would enjoy it too, we'd love to hear from you:

facebook.com/4ingredientspage

4 Ingredients Channel

@4ingredients

@4ingredients

@4ingredients

4ingredients.com.au

People who bought 4 Ingredients KETO also bought:

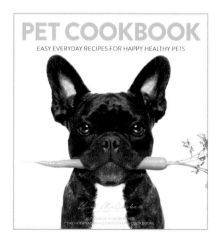

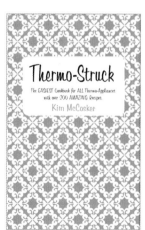

Bibliography

Websites

Foodworks 9 Professional
For all Nutritional Calculations
https://xyris.com.au/thanks-for-trying-foodworks/

How the Ketogenic Diet Weakens Cancer Cells.
Article Summary extract (P. 4)
https://thetruthaboutcancer.com/ketogenic-diet-weakens-cancer-cells/

Is Keto for me?
https://www.dietdoctor.com/low-carb/keto

Keto Diet Food List
www.ketosummit.com

Keto Plate inspiration from
http://www.higheeledmummy.com

Books & Magazines

Health Benefits of Walking
(P. 13). Prevention Magazine.
Published January, 2015.

McCosker, Kim. *4 Ingredients HEALTHY DIET.* 4 Ingredients. PO BOX 400. Caloundra Queensland 4551. Australia.

McCosker, Kim. *4 Ingredients MORE Gluten Free Lactose Free.* 4 Ingredients. PO BOX 400. Caloundra Queensland 4551. Australia.

30 DAYS FROM NOW YOU'LL THANK YOURSELF

METRIC CONVERSION CHARTS

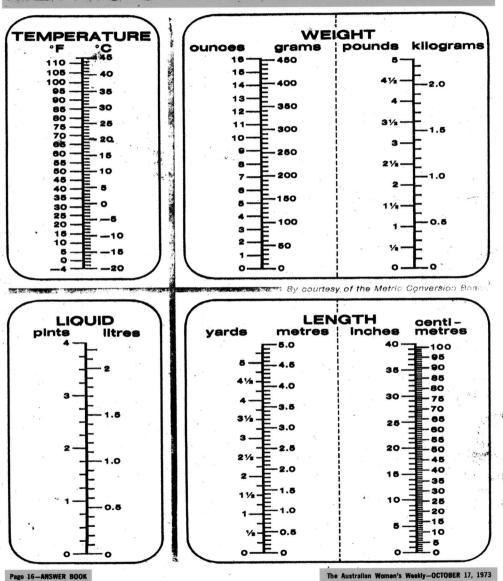

TEMPERATURE

°F	°C
110	45
105	40
100	
95	35
90	
85	30
80	
75	25
70	20
65	
60	15
55	
50	10
45	
40	5
35	
30	0
25	
20	—5
15	
10	—10
5	—15
0	
—4	—20

WEIGHT

ounces	grams	pounds	kilograms
16	450	5	
15			
14	400	4½	2.0
13			
12	350	4	
11	300	3½	1.5
10			
9	250	3	
8		2½	
7	200		1.0
6		2	
5	150		
4	100	1½	
3		1	0.5
2	50		
1		½	
0	0	0	0

By courtesy of the Metric Conversion Board

LIQUID

pints	litres
4	
	2
3	
	1.5
2	1.0
1	0.5
0	0

LENGTH

yards	metres	inches	centi-metres
	5.0	40	100
5	4.5	35	95 / 90 / 85
4½	4.0		80
4	3.5	30	75 / 70
3½	3.0	25	65 / 60 / 55
3	2.5	20	50 / 45
2½	2.0		40 / 35
2	1.5	15	30
1½	1.0	10	25 / 20
1			15
½	0.5	5	10 / 5
0	0	0	0

Printed by Conpress Printing Ltd., of 168 Castlereagh St., Sydney, at 61-63 O'Riordan St., Alexandria.

141

Index

What is Keto? 3

Why Keto? 4

Is Keto for me? 5

Keto Dients are Great and Even Easy 6

Keto Friendly Foods 8

Keto Unfriendly Foods. 11

Water. 12

Walking 13

The Keto Plate. 14

A Typical Day on the Keto Diet 15

Guide to Weights & Measures 16

TABLE OF CONTENTS. 17

KETO FRIENDLY BREAKFASTS. 18

Baked Eggs in Tomatoes. 20

Breakfast Quiches 22

Breakfast STACK 24

Classic KETO Breakfast 26

EASY Boiled Eggs. 28

Eggs 'n' Peppers 30

Herbed Omelette 32

KETO Pancakes 34

OMEGA-ME Puddings. 36

Strawberry Chia Pudding 38

Waffles 40

KETO FRIENDLY SMOOTHIES 42

Delicious Keto Iced Coffee. 42

Green Goddess 43

Strawberry Avocado Smoothie 43

KETO FRIENDLY SNACKS. 44

Asparagus Wraps 46

Caprese Bites. 48

Cucumber Tuna Bites 50

Devilled Eggs. 52

EASY French Onion Dip 54

KETO Crackers. 56

KETO Grazing Platter. 58

Parmesan Crisps 60

Pink Pickled Onions 62

Ricotta & Prosciutto Baked Pies. 64

KETO FRIENDLY DRESSINGS 66

2-Ingredient Sauerkraut. 66

Avocado Coriander Lime Mayonnaise. 66

Basil Pesto 66

EASY Blue Cheese Dressing 67

Classic Salad Dressing 67

Seafood Sauce 67

KETO FRIENDLY LUNCHES **68**

Creamy Tomato Soup 70

Egg Caper Salad 72

Prawn Cocktail 74

Salmon Omelette Rolls 76

Salmon Timbale 78

Spinach & Feta Cakes 80

Thai Chicken Patties 82

Zucchini Pizzas 84

KETO FRIENDLY DINNERS **86**

Baked Ricotta Pie 88

Basil Pesto Frittata 90

Blue Cheese Pork with Asparagus 92

Chicken, Mushroom & Pesto Stack 94

Greek Lamb Meatballs 96

Green Chicken Curry 98

Grilled Fish with Tartare Sauce 100

Mediterranean Rosemary Skewers 102

Mediterranean Stuffed Capsicums 104

Prawns with Creamy Dipping Sauce 106

Salmon BLT 108

Salmon Pesto Salad 110

San Choi Bau 112

Satay Pork Skewers 114

Slow Cooked Lamb with Onions & Rosemary 116

Steak with Creamy Mushroom Sauce 118

Texan Pork Chops 120

KETO FRIENDLY SWEETIES **122**

Berry Parfaits 124

Cheesecake KETO Bombs 126

CocoAvo Ice-cream Cake 127

Coconut Yoghurt with Walnuts & Spices 128

Cinnamon Dip 129

ChocCado Truffles 130

Pistachio Crusted Truffles 131

Frozen Fat Bombs 132

Strawberry Fields Forever 134

Shortbread Cookies 136

Strawberry & PB Fudge 137

Nuts About These 137

Please Join Us 138

BIBLIOGRAPHY **140**

Metric Conversion Charts 141

INDEX **142**

KETO FOODS

LOW CARBS
VEGETABLES
GOOD MEATS
HEALTHY FATS
SEAFOOD & FISH